Slim Goodbody's
Life Skills
101

WHAT SHOULD I DO?

Making Good Decisions

Crabtree Publishing Company
www.crabtreebooks.com

Series Development, Writing, and Packaging:
John Burstein, Slim Goodbody Corp.

Editors:
Reagan Miller, Valerie Weber, and Mark Sachner,
Water Buffalo Books

Proofreader:
Molly Aloian

Editorial director:
Kathy Middleton

Production coordinator:
Kenneth Wright

Prepress technicians:
Margaret Amy Salter, Kenneth Wright

Designer: Tammy West, Westgraphix LLC.

Photos: Chris Pinchback, Pinchback Photography

"Slim Goodbody" and Pinchback photos, copyright,
© Slim Goodbody

Photo credits:
Shutterstock: p. 4 (middle, bottom), 5 (middle,
bottom), 6 (middle, bottom, left), 7 (all), 9 (bottom),
11 (top), 18, 19 (top)
© Slim Goodbody: p. 1, 4 (top), 5 (top), 6 (top),
8 (all), 9 (top), 10, 11 (middle, bottom), 12, 13,
14, 15, 16, 17, 19 (bottom), 20, 21, 22, 23, 24, 25,
26, 27, 28, 29

Acknowledgements:
The author would like to thank the following
children for all their help in this project: Stephanie
Bartlett , Sarah Booth, Christine Burstein, Lucas
Burstein, Olivia Davis, Eleni Fernald, Kylie Fong,
Tristan Fong, Colby Hill, Carrie Laurita, Ginny
Lauria, Henry Laurita, Louis Laurita, Nathan
Levig, Havana Lyman, Renaissance Lyman,
Andrew McBride, Lulu McClure, Yanmei
McElhaney, Amanda Mirabile, Esme Power, Emily
Pratt, Andrew Smith, Dylan Smith, Mary Wells

"Slim Goodbody" and "Slim Goodbody's Life
Skills 101" are registered trademarks of the Slim
Goodbody Corp.

Library and Archives Canada Cataloguing in Publication

Burstein, John
    What should I do? : making good decisions / John Burstein.

(Slim Goodbody's life skills 101)
Includes index.
ISBN 978-0-7787-4791-8 (bound).--ISBN 978-0-7787-4807-6 (pbk.)

    1. Decision making--Juvenile literature. I. Title. II. Title: Making good
decisions. III. Series: Burstein, John. Slim Goodbody's life skills 101

BF723.D34B87 2010   j153.8'3   C2009-903736-X

Library of Congress Cataloging-in-Publication Data

Burstein, John.
    What should I do? : making good decisions / John Burstein.
      p. cm. -- (Slim Goodbody's life skills 101)
    Includes index.
    ISBN 978-0-7787-4807-6 (pbk. : alk. paper) -- ISBN 978-0-7787-4791-8 (reinforced
library binding : alk. paper)
    1. Decision making--Juvenile literature. 2. Problem solving--Juvenile literature.
I. Title. II. Series.

    BF441.B94 2009
    153.8'3--dc22

    2009023635

Published in Canada
Crabtree Publishing
616 Welland Ave.
St. Catharines, Ontario
L2M 5V6

Published in the United States
Crabtree Publishing
PMB16A
350 Fifth Ave., Suite 3308
New York, NY 10118

Published in the United Kingdom
Crabtree Publishing
White Cross Mills
High Town, Lancaster
LA1 4XS

Published in Australia
Crabtree Publishing
386 Mt. Alexander Rd.
Ascot Vale (Melbourne)
VIC 3032

CONTENTS

THE CHOICE IS YOURS...................4

THOUSANDS AND THOUSANDS 6

BIG AND SMALL 8

BRAIN DIVIDE 10

SKILL ONE: STOP AND BREATHE 12

SKILL TWO: COLLECT THE FACTS............14

SKILL THREE: NOW OR LATER?...............16

SKILL FOUR: KNOW YOUR GOAL.............18

SKILL FIVE: EXPLORE YOUR OPTIONS....20

SKILL SIX: CONSIDER THE CONSEQUENCES....22

SKILL SEVEN: TAKE ACTION 24

SKILL EIGHT: REVIEW THE RESULTS 26

FOLLOW YOUR OWN PATH....................28

GLOSSARY 30

FOR MORE INFORMATION 31

INDEX 32

Words in **bold** are defined
in the glossary on page 30.

THE CHOICE IS YOURS

Kendra was feeling confused and upset. Her stomach even felt tight and a little sore.

It was Thursday evening. She had just finished talking on the phone with her friend Ian. Ian had invited her to go to the circus on Saturday. Kendra said she would ask her parents for **permission** to go and call right back. The circus came to town only once every couple of years. Kendra really wanted to go, but there was a problem. She had already promised to go to the movies with her friend Samantha on Saturday. Kendra knew Samantha was really looking forward to going. They had been talking about it all week long.

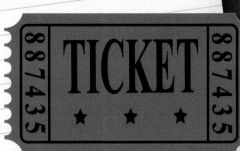

She didn't want to hurt Samantha's feelings. But Kendra also wanted to go to the circus a lot more than to the movies. Now she was stuck.

Or was she? "I could call Samantha and say I changed my mind," she thought. "But is that fair?"

Kendra had no idea what to do! She knew that she had to make a decision. But how was she ever going to make it?

Hi. My name is Slim Goodbody.

I wrote this book to help you learn how to make good decisions. Decision making is one of the most important skills you can develop. You'll use it your entire life. Good decision-making skills help you make smart choices. Smart choices help you become a healthy, happy person.

Sometimes making a decision may seem like too much work. But deciding things yourself is the only way to be in control of your life.

Practice Makes Perfect

Every new skill takes practice, from playing soccer to playing the piano. Decision-making skills are no different. As you practice making decisions, you'll probably make a few mistakes. But don't worry. Every decision gives you a chance to learn and grow. Each time that you make a mistake, you gain more knowledge about yourself and others. This information will help you make better decisions in the future.

THOUSANDS AND THOUSANDS

During your life, you will make thousands and thousands of decisions. Think about how many decisions you make in just one day! Here are just a few things you might decide:

- What clothes to wear
- What to eat for breakfast
- Where to sit on the bus
- Where to sit at lunchtime
- Whether to raise your hand in class
  - How long to study
  - What book to read
  - What game to play at recess
  - Who to play with after school
  - When to do your homework
  - What TV show to watch
- What music to listen to

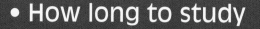

Moment by Moment

The list of things you decide is actually endless. Moment by moment, day by day, new **situations** come up. Each situation may require new decisions. For example, here's a decision I want you to make right now:

Will you read the next sentence in my book?

If you decided, "Yes, I will," then you are reading this sentence. If you put the book down, I guess you decided, "No, I won't."

Keep Count

Carry a notebook around with you for one day. Whenever you have a chance, write down the decisions that you've already made. You can write down the decisions that you think you'll make later on. At the end of the day, count up how many decisions you've made.

BIG AND SMALL

Not every decision you make is a big deal. Many decisions are small and simple to make. A small decision might be deciding which socks to put on in the morning or whether to eat an apple or a banana after school.

Bigger Decisions

We won't be dealing with these kinds of decisions in this book. Small decisions don't usually matter much when it comes to your health and happiness. Instead, I want to **focus** on bigger and more important decisions. For example, the kind of decisions you make

- if you're thinking about breaking a promise to a friend;
- if a friend does something risky and wants you to join in;
- if telling the truth will get you into trouble;
- if you're mad at a friend for hurting your feelings.

Lose or Keep

Making these types of decisions can have a big effect on your life. Depending upon your choice, you could lose or keep a friendship. More importantly, depending upon your choice, you could lose or keep your own **self-respect**. Self-respect is feeling good about the kind of person you are deep down inside.

Confusion

Making important decisions can often be confusing. One of the reasons for this **confusion** has a lot to do with how your brain works.

BRAIN DIVIDE

The thinking part of your brain is called the **cerebrum**. Some areas of your cerebrum deal with facts. Other areas of your cerebrum deal with feelings.

Most important decisions involve both the facts and feelings areas of your brain. These two areas don't always **evaluate**, or "see things," in the same way. Let me give you two examples:

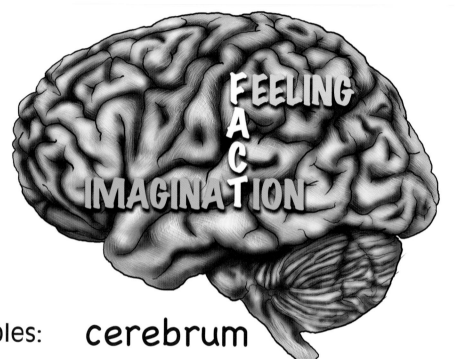

cerebrum

• Imagine that your friend asks to copy your homework. The fact area of your brain might think, "Copying is wrong. It can get me in trouble. I'll say no!" The feeling area might disagree and think, "It feels good to help a friend, so I'll say yes!"

• Imagine that your sister wants your help on her math homework. The fact area of your brain might think, "I understand how to do these problems. I'll say yes." The feeling area might disagree and think, "My sister is always bugging me. I don't feel like helping out. I'll say no."

Imagine This

To make decision making even more confusing, your cerebrum has a powerful ability called **imagination**. Imagination allows people to do wonderful things. With their imagination, people can write stories, play games of make-believe, and create new inventions. Imagination can also lead you to believe something that isn't true.

Imagine that a friend doesn't call you when she said she would. You might think that she is angry at you. Your feelings might be hurt. Later, though, you find out she was sick and had to go see a doctor. You then realize you felt hurt because you imagined something that wasn't true.

This Way and That

feelings

When facts, feelings, and imagination are pulling this way and that, people can have trouble making good decisions. They may also think that they don't have time to make up their minds. What if it's your decision? What can you do about this problem? You can begin with decision-making skill one.

facts

imagination

SKILL ONE: STOP AND BREATHE

The first decision-making skill is pretty simple. Before you start—stop!

You read me correctly. Before making any decision, stop. Take a deep breath. Give yourself a chance to relax for a moment. Taking a little time allows you to

- **consider** the facts;
- check your feelings;
- control your imagination.

A short pause and a deep breath will help your mind settle down. When you start making a decision, you want to be as calm as possible.

STOP AND BREATHE

Is There a Choice?

Once you've taken a short break, ask yourself the following question.

"Can I actually do anything about this situation?"

In other words, even if you could make a decision, would it matter? Maybe it would, maybe it wouldn't. Let me give you an example. Suppose one morning, you wake up a little tired, and you don't want to go to school.

Would your parents actually give you a choice about going to school? Could you decide not to go? I'll bet this decision is not up to you. Since you don't have the power to decide, thinking about what decision to make is a waste of time. You might as well just get up, get dressed, and get going. On the other hand, if you believe your decision would count, it's time to take the next step.

SKILL TWO: COLLECT THE FACTS

It often takes time to clearly understand the details of a situation. To **grasp** a situation, you need to collect the facts. If you don't understand what's happening, how can you decide what to do about it? For example, suppose you got into an argument with a good friend during a baseball game.

Begin by asking yourself two questions:

- What happened?
- Who was involved?

Write down your answers to these questions. Try to state the situation as clearly as possible.

Now dig a little deeper and ask yourself:

- How did it start?
- Why do I think it happened?

You will probably need to use your imagination to come up with some of the answers.

Check Your Feelings

Once you've collected the facts, check on your feelings, Ask yourself:

- How do I feel about what happened?

If other people were involved, you can ask them these questions, too. Some people may even disagree about exactly what happened. But the more information you learn, the better the decision you'll be able to make.

gut feeling

What's Your Hunch?

You can never know for sure exactly why someone else acts in a certain way. As you answer the questions above, pay attention to any **hunches** you might have. A hunch is sometimes called a "gut feeling." A hunch isn't based on facts. It's an inner sense that you understand something even if you can't quite explain why. In most cases, you can trust your hunches.

Once you understand the situation better, you're ready to take the next step.

SKILL THREE: NOW OR LATER?

Think about the timing. Just because a decision can be made right away does not mean it should be made right away. Many situations don't require "now-or-never" choices. Instead of making a quick decision, ask yourself, "Do I have to decide right now?"

Often, it's smarter to wait awhile. Waiting will give you a chance to gather more information. For example, you might have time to talk with others who may be able to help you. When you have more information, you will have a far better chance of making a good decision.

Decision Dangers

The major problem with quick decisions is that they usually lead to taking quick actions. As long as you're still thinking about what to do, you can still change your mind if necessary. Once you act on a decision, you cannot erase that action. Acting too quickly can cause you to

- lose friends;
- make mistakes;
- get hurt;
- make the situation worse;
- get into trouble;
- feel bad about yourself.

If you make a mistake, you may be able to apologize. You may promise not to do it again. But you can't undo what you did. What's done is done.

If you are ready to go ahead and make a decision, be sure to practice the next decision-making skill first.

SKILL FOUR: KNOW YOUR GOAL

When you know most of the facts, you're almost ready to make a decision. First, however, you need to know your goal. Your goal is how you want the situation to end. For example, if you were running a race, your goal would be reaching the finish line. If you were shooting hoops, your goal would be sinking the shot. To discover your goal in a confusing situation, it helps to ask yourself,

"If I could get exactly what I wanted in this situation, what would that be?"

If you are upset about something, you may not be thinking clearly. When your goal is unclear, it may help to talk things over with your parents, teachers, or friends.

Deciding Your Direction

When you know what you want, it's easier to figure out how to get there! Imagine you're riding your bike. If your goal is to go home, you'll decide to travel in a certain direction. If your goal is to go to the store, you'll decide to travel in another direction. When you know where you want to go, you can avoid making a lot of wrong turns.

Whenever you are faced with an important decision, always ask yourself first, "What is my goal?" The answer to that question will lead you in one direction or another.

A Fight with a Friend

Imagine you have a fight with a friend. If your goal is to end your friendship, you may decide not to call your friend ever again. If your goal is to stay friends, you might decide to call your friend right away to talk about the fight.

Once you know your goal, it's time to take the next step.

SKILL FIVE: EXPLORE YOUR OPTIONS

There are usually several ways to reach a goal, so explore your **options**. We can use the bike ride example to explore our options. If your goal is to reach home, you will probably have different choices of how to get there. You can travel on different streets. Some streets may get you home faster, but you would have to bike with cars speeding past you. Other streets may take longer to travel, but they are safer and quieter. Knowing your options helps you find the very best way to reach your goal. So before making a decision:

- Come up with as many options as possible for reaching your goal.

- Use your imagination. Don't stop to think if your ideas are **practical** or not.

- Ask your family, teachers, and friends for any ideas they have.

- Write down every option that comes to mind. The more possibilities you have, the better.

Limit Your List

When your list is complete, read it over. Cross out any options that you think couldn't work because they

- are silly or dumb;
- are impossible to do;
- would take too long;
- would involve too many people;
- are selfish or mean;
- are unsafe and could lead to a dangerous situation.

Once an option is crossed off, don't waste any more time thinking about it. Now ask yourself, "Which of the options left would best help me solve the problem?"

Delaying or Doing Nothing

Do not forget that one option may be to do nothing. Sometimes it's best to hold off on doing something because you think that

- you don't have enough information to choose wisely;
- with more time, you'll be able to gather more facts;
- doing nothing is better than any other option;
- you can't think clearly until you have calmed down.

To help you figure out the best option, take the next step.

SKILL SIX: CONSIDER THE CONSEQUENCES

Consider the **consequences** for each of the options on your list. The word "consequence" means what is likely to happen if you act on an option. For each option, think about

- what can go right and what can go wrong;
- what you could gain and what you could lose.

You may think an option is good at first. After considering the consequences, however, you might realize it wouldn't be a wise choice.

Pros and Cons

One way to figure out consequences is to write down the **pros** and **cons** for each option. The pros are positive results you think can happen. The cons are the negative results.

Here are some examples of pros:

- I will feel proud of myself.
- It's simple to do.
- It can be done quickly.
- It will make me happy.
- It's honest and fair.
- I can keep my friends.
- My parents will respect my actions.

Here are some examples of cons:

- I can get into trouble.
- I can hurt myself or others.
- It might make the situation worse.
- My parents will be upset.
- It will be hard for others to trust me again.
- I will let people down.

After studying the pros and cons, you'll probably find it easier to pick an option. If not, talk the situation over with your parents, teacher, or other trusted adult. They can help you choose the option that gives you the best chance to reach your goal.

SKILL SEVEN: TAKE ACTION

Now that you know what you want to do, be sure you do it as well as you can. When you make a decision, you can never be completely sure that your choice will work out. To give yourself the best chance of success, write down your plan of action. Include these points:

- when and where you will begin;
- if you will ask for any help;
- whom you will ask for help.

Take some time to review your action plan. When you put your plan down on paper, you might see a few changes you want to make. When you are satisfied with your plan and the time is right, go for it!

Be Brave

Be brave and follow through on your decision. Give it your best effort.

Trust Yourself

All big decisions involve some risk. Without taking risks, you cannot learn or improve. It is important you trust that you've made the best decision that you could. You should also trust that you'll be able to handle the consequences. Remember, it's okay if things don't work out exactly as planned. After all, when you were considering the consequences, you were only imagining what was likely to happen. You couldn't actually know what would happen. With all the work you've done, though, the chances are good your decision will work out for the best.

SKILL EIGHT: REVIEW THE RESULTS

After taking action, you need to review the results. Reviewing what happened gives you the chance to see if you made a good choice. Reviewing also gives you information that can help you if you are faced with a similar situation in the future.

Ask yourself these questions:

- How well did things work out?
- Was there something more that I could have done?
- Has the problem been fixed?
- Did my choice help me reach my goal?
- Would I decide differently the next time?

Even if your decision didn't work out perfectly, be proud that you did your best.

Try, Try Again

You probably know the old expression, "If at first you don't succeed, try, try again." This **advice** also applies to the decisions you make. If the option you acted on didn't work out, you might have a chance to try again. If you don't have the **opportunity** right away, at least you learned something that can help you in the future.

Problems as Opportunities

Try to see problems and decisions as opportunities to learn more about yourself. For example, if a friend asks you to play a mean joke on someone, you will be faced with a decision. As you work your way through different options, you will discover more about what you truly value. You will then have the opportunity to make a choice that will make you feel proud of yourself.

FOLLOW YOUR OWN PATH

Everyone is different. No two people will make the same decisions. Your friends may choose one thing and you might choose another. The most important thing is to be true to yourself. Your decisions should be based on who you are inside and what matters most to you. Do not go along with the crowd. Follow your own path.

Learn the List

You have now learned about eight decision-making skills. To help you remember them, here is a list. Review these skills. Think about how you can use them next time you're faced with an important decision.

A Fast Decision

Sometimes, you might have to make a choice quickly. You won't have time to think through all eight steps. But by practicing these steps when you can, you'll learn how good decision making works and feels. You'll be able to make better fast decisions, too.

Skill One: Stop and Breathe

Skill Two: Collect the Facts

Skill Three: Now or Later?

Skill Four: Know Your Goal

Skill Five: Explore Your Options

Skill Six: Consider the Consequences

Skill Seven: Take Action

Skill Eight: Review the Results

Now You Know

You will be making decisions for the rest of your life. As you practice your decision-making skills, you will get better at them. The better your skills are, the healthier and happier you will be. I'd like to ask you to make a decision right now! Decide to start practicing your skills the next time you have an important decision to make.

GLOSSARY

advice Thoughts about what could or should be done

cerebrum The large front or upper part of your brain

confusion Disorder; mix-up

cons Disadvantages or bad results of doing something

consequences Results; outcomes

consider To take into account something; to think about

evaluate To decide the worth of something; to decide whether something is wrong or right

focus To pay attention to; to direct attention to

grasp To understand what is happening

hunches Guesses or thoughts about something

imagination The ability to create new ideas or images

opportunity Chance or favorable time

options Chances; choices

permission Refers to agreeing to let someone do something

practical Describes something that can be done, something that is sensible

pros Advantages or good results of doing something

self-respect The honor and regard you should have for yourself and your character

situations The way things are; conditions

BOOKS

How to Say No and Keep Your Friends: Peer Pressure Reversal for Teens and Preteens. Sharon Scott. HRD Press.

PeerPressure: Deal with it without losing your cool. Elaine Slavens (Author), Ben Shannon (Illustrator). Lorimer.

Stick Up for Yourself: Every Kid's Guide to Personal Power & Positive Self-Esteem. Gershen Kaufman (Author), Lev Raphael (Author), Pamela Espeland (Author). Free Spirit Publishing.

Hot Issues, Cool Choices: Facing Bullies, Peer Pressure, Popularity, and Put-downs. Sandra McLeod Humphrey (Author), Brian Strassburg (Illustrator). Prometheus Books.

WEB SITES

The Cool Spot
www.thecoolspot.gov/pressures.asp
Watch videos, play games, and learn a lot about risky behavior, peer pressure, and how to make good choices.

Kidshealth
kidshealth.org/kid/feeling/friend/peer_pressure.html
Check out this Web site for information on how to deal with peer pressure.

Kids' Health: Child and Youth Health
www.cyh.com/HealthTopics/HealthTopicDetailsKids.aspx?p=335&np=286&id=1822
Visit this Web site to learn about making good choices and resisting peer pressure. You can also play games and read what other kids have to say about staying healthy.

Slim Goodbody
www.slimgoodbody.com
Discover loads of fun and free downloads for kids, teachers, and parents.

INDEX

Brain 9, 10–11
Breathing 12, 29

Cerebrum 10–11
Choices, making 5, 9, 13, 15, 17, 24, 26, 27, 29
Confusion 4, 9, 11, 18
Consequences, considering 22–23, 25, 29

Dangers 17, 21
  See also Risk, taking a
Direction, deciding 19

Facts, collecting and dealing with 10, 11, 12, 14–15, 18, 21, 29
Feelings
  Dealing with 10–11, 12
  Hurt 4, 8
Friends and friendship 4, 8, 9, 10, 11, 14, 17, 18, 19, 20, 23, 27, 28

Goal, knowing and reaching your 18, 19, 20, 23, 26, 29

Hunches 15

Imagination and imagining 11, 12, 14, 20, 25
Information, gaining 5, 15, 16, 21, 26

Keeping count 7

Mistakes, making 5, 17

Options, exploring 20–21, 22, 23, 29

Parents 4, 13, 18, 23
Permission, asking for 4
Promises 4, 8, 17
Pros and cons 23

Reviewing actions and results 24, 26, 28, 29
Risk, taking a 8, 25
  See also Dangers

Self-respect 9
Skills, decision-making 5, 11, 12–13, 14–15, 16–17, 18–19, 20–21, 22–23, 24–25, 26–27, 28, 29

Taking action 17, 24–25, 26, 29
Teachers 13, 18, 23
Thinking clearly 18, 21
Trouble, getting into 8, 10, 17, 23
Trusting yourself 15, 25

Waiting 16

About the Author
John Burstein (also known as Slim Goodbody) has been entertaining and educating children for over thirty years. His programs have been broadcast on CBS, PBS, Nickelodeon, USA, and Discovery. He has won numerous awards including the Parent's Choice Award and the President's Council's Fitness Leader Award. Currently, Mr. Burstein tours the country with his multimedia live show "Bodyology." For more information, please visit **slimgoodbody.com**.

Printed in the U.S.A.— CG